UNBREAKABLE
BECOMING ANTIFRAGILE

JAMES BECTON

FORWARD

In the vast tapestry of existence, we are bound to encounter storms, tumultuous winds that threaten to uproot our very foundations. Life, in its infinite wisdom, often sends surges of uncertainty our way, challenging us to not just survive but to thrive amidst the chaos. It is here, in the crucible of life's upheavals, that we find ourselves confronted with a choice—a choice to merely endure the storm or to rise, stronger and more resilient, because of them.

As we stand on the precipice of a new decade, the landscape before us is unlike any we've witnessed before. The winds of change blow with an unprecedented force, shaking the very bedrock of our existence. In the face of such unrelenting disruption, our traditional notions of resilience, of merely bouncing back, have begun to falter. The demands of this era are different; they call for something more profound, something enduring.

This book is an invitation to transcend the confines of mere resilience and step into the realm of antifragility. It beckons us to not merely withstand the storms but to harness their power for our own growth and empowerment. It is a journey into the heart of change, a quest to find strength in adversity, and a promise that we can not only weather the storms but emerge from them, forged anew and **Unbreakable.**

Drawing from the rich tapestry of neuroscience, psychology, and the lived experiences of countless individuals, this book offers a guiding light through the labyrinth of uncertainty. It presents not a shield against life's disruptions but a sword—a tool to cut through the chaos and carve a path toward becoming antifragile.

Within these pages, you will discover the art of embracing change, of leaning into challenges with an unwavering spirit, and of flourishing when the world tests your resolve. It is a testament to the unyielding human spirit and the limitless potential that resides within each of us.

So, as you embark on this transformative journey, remember this: in every storm, in every trial, there lies an opportunity—a chance to not just survive but to thrive, to emerge unbreakable. You hold in your hands the map to that uncharted territory, and it is my sincerest hope that you embrace it with an open heart and an indomitable spirit.

Let us navigate the uncertain waters ahead together, for it is in our shared journey that we find the strength to **Become Antifragile.**

CONTENTS

INTRODUCTION

In a world constantly shifting and filled with uncertainties, where challenges loom at every turn, there lies an extraordinary journey awaiting those who dare to embrace a concept as powerful as it is transformative: the art of antifragility.

Coined by none other than the eminent professor, former trader, and hedge fund manager Nassim Nicholas Taleb, antifragility is not merely the capacity to endure the shocks of life; it's the profound ability to thrive because of them. The beacon of hope beckons us to rise above the tumultuous tides and emerge not just unscathed but stronger and more resolute.

Welcome to **Unbreakable: Becoming Antifragile**, a compelling and illuminating exploration of this revolutionary idea. Within these pages, we embark on a captivating journey that guides us through life's intricate maze. We'll uncover the very essence of antifragility. This philosophy unveils its secrets not through complex theories but through the riveting stories of ordinary individuals who, against all odds, have reshaped their destinies.

These stories serve as beacons of inspiration, proving that life's trials and tribulations are not stumbling blocks but steppingstones to empowerment and growth. From personal relationships to the pinnacle of professional success, from nurturing physical well-being to fortifying mental resilience, **Unbreakable** offers more than just wisdom; it provides actionable strategies.

Drawing upon a wellspring of knowledge that spans ancient philosophies to the cutting-edge insights of modern psychology, this book forms a comprehensive guide. It serves as a compass in the turbulent sea of uncertainty, ensuring that as you embark on this transformative voyage, you will uncover a remarkable truth: the power to not only weather life's storms but to emerge from them unbreakable in spirit.

So, my fellow traveler, as we set sail on this extraordinary voyage through the pages of this book, know this: adversity is not your journey's end; it is, in fact, the very genesis of your boundless potential. Welcome to the beginning of your voyage into antifragility.

CHAPTER
1
EMBRACING
ANTIFRAGILITY

ANTIFRAGILE

Adj: Objects, people, or properties that
improve with chaos and disorder.

The opposite of fragile, it is often confused
with robustness, resilience, or strength.
However, while these are merely indifferent
to chaos and disorder, Antifragile things
relish, improve, and otherwise benefit from
chaos and disorder.

n the swirling currents of our ever-changing world, we frequently find ourselves adrift in the uncharted waters of uncertainty, buffeted by the turbulent winds of adversity. Life's challenges resemble the unrelenting tides, at times gentle and at times fierce, yet a constant presence. It is within this capricious ocean of existence that we encounter the profound concept of antifragility—a guiding light that offers not merely survival but the promise of thriving amid tumultuous seas.

As we embark on this transformative journey, it is imperative to first grasp the essence of antifragility. This concept was coined by Nassim Nicholas Taleb, a luminary whose insights have guided numerous individuals in their quest for resilience and fortitude.

Understanding Nassim Taleb's Antifragility Framework

In the opening chapter of our journey into the world of antifragility, we step into the intellectual realm crafted by the remarkable Nassim Taleb. Taleb, a distinguished figure known for his roles as an author, philosopher, and risk analyst, has made an enduring impact through his groundbreaking work on antifragility. His contributions have fundamentally reshaped our perspectives on how we should understand and effectively respond to the ever-present uncertainty and volatility that define our complex world.

At the heart of this chapter lies Taleb's Antifragility Framework, which serves as the bedrock for our exploration. It equips us with the essential concepts needed to grasp the essence of becoming antifragile. Within these pages, we'll delve into the critical elements of Taleb's framework and explore how they shape our understanding of various systems, whether they are financial markets, businesses, or our personal lives. Antifragility transcends mere theory; it stands as a guiding philosophy, an ethos that propels us beyond the mere struggle for survival and into the realm of growing and thriving.

As we journey through this chapter, you will build a solid foundation in Taleb's Antifragility Framework. This foundation is essential for appreciating the transformative potential of antifragility as we navigate our ever-evolving world. The wisdom contained in Taleb's work acts as a guiding light for the transformative voyage that awaits us in our exploration of antifragility.

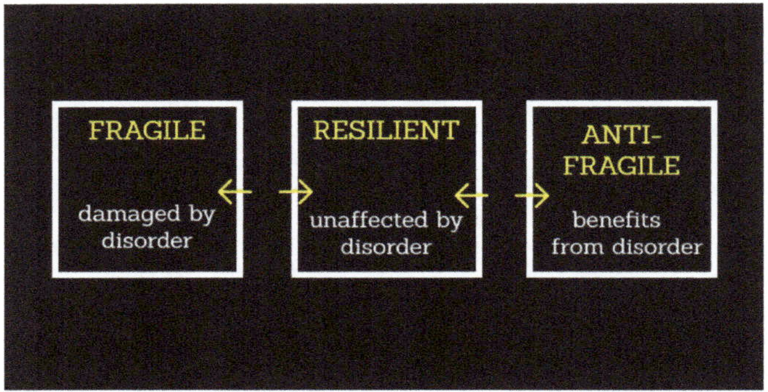

- **Fragility vs. Antifragility**: Taleb introduces the central idea of the fragility-antifragility spectrum, where systems are classified into three categories: fragile, resilient, and antifragile. Fragile systems are vulnerable to shocks and disruptions, while resilient systems can withstand them without being affected. Antifragile systems, on the other hand, thrive and improve in the face of adversity. We dissect these distinctions, helping you grasp the nuances that distinguish these categories.

- **Randomness and Uncertainty**: Taleb's work emphasizes the role of randomness and uncertainty in our lives. We explore how embracing randomness as an inherent part of existence can lead to a more profound understanding of antifragility.

- **Skin in the Game**: Another critical component of Taleb's framework is the idea of "skin in the game." He argues that true accountability and antifragility are achieved when individuals and organizations have a personal stake in the outcomes of their decisions. We delve into the implications of this concept, illustrating how it can be applied in various contexts.

- **Optionality and Convexity**: Taleb's insights into optionality and convexity are essential aspects of his antifragility framework. We explore how having multiple options and asymmetric payoffs can enhance resilience and adaptability in the face of uncertainty.

Now, let's imagine for a moment a fragile object—a delicate vase, perhaps. When subjected to the slightest jolt, it shatters into irreparable pieces. Fragility is the state of vulnerability, where even the slightest disturbance can result in catastrophic consequences. Many aspects of our lives, similar to fragile vases, are susceptible to breaking when faced with adversity.

Now, envision something different—a phoenix rising from the ashes, emerging stronger and more vibrant than before. This is the essence of antifragility. It's the concept that when confronted with challenges, setbacks, and shocks, we don't merely endure; we emerge from the crucible of adversity as more robust and resilient beings.

Nassim Taleb likens it to the ancient mythological creature, the Hydra. When one of its heads is severed, two more grow in its place. The Hydra thrives on whatever tries to destroy it, and so can we. The storms of life that threaten to upend our existence can, instead, become the very nourishment that fuels our growth.

As we embark on this journey of self-discovery and empowerment, let's remember that we are not delicate vases meant to break at the slightest adversity. Rather, we are like potential phoenixes, able to rise from life's challenges with newfound strength and unwavering determination. In the upcoming chapters, we will discover how to ignite the unbreakable spirit within us and become the creators of our own antifragility.

CHAPTER
2
THE NATURE
OF ADVERSITY

Within the grand tapestry of life, adversity weaves itself seamlessly into the very fabric of our existence. It is a thread that, upon first glance, may appear dark and foreboding, yet upon closer examination, reveals its intricate and transformative beauty.

Adversity, that steadfast companion on our human journey, frequently makes its entrance uninvited. It manifests in various forms, from the subtle ripples of inconvenience to the tempestuous storms of tragedy. However, irrespective of its appearance, adversity serves a purpose that extends far beyond mere disruption. It is the vessel within which the transformation of personal growth takes place.

The Psychology of Resilience: How Individuals Respond to Adversity

Within the pages of the second chapter of our exploration into antifragility, we venture deep into the heart of adversity. Adversity is a force that we all encounter at some point in our lives, and it is in these challenging moments that the true nature of our resilience is revealed. This chapter is dedicated to unraveling the intricate psychology of resilience, shedding light on how individuals respond when faced with life's formidable trials.

Resilience, the capacity to endure and rebound from adversity, forms the cornerstone of our investigation. We peel back the layers of this essential trait, seeking to comprehend its underlying mechanisms. Drawing from a blend of psychological research findings and real-life narratives, we gain profound insights into the multifaceted ways individuals react when confronted with adversity.

- **Coping Mechanisms**: Our journey begins with a closer examination of the diverse coping mechanisms that individuals employ to navigate adversity. Some may turn to social support networks, drawing strength from their connections with loved ones. Others might develop personal strategies for managing stress and finding hope amidst chaos. Through the study of these mechanisms, we uncover how individuals harness their inner resources to confront adversity head-on.

- **Adaptive vs. Maladaptive Responses**: We delve into the crucial distinction between adaptive and maladaptive responses to adversity. Adaptive responses encompass constructive actions and shifts in mindset that enable individuals not only to endure adversity but to emerge from it stronger. Conversely, maladaptive responses can perpetuate suffering and hinder personal growth. Understanding this distinction equips us with the knowledge needed to foster resilience effectively.

- **Post-Traumatic Growth**: One remarkable facet of resilience is the potential for post-traumatic growth. We explore the concept that adversity can serve as a catalyst for profound personal transformation. Through real-life stories of individuals who have experienced trauma and emerged with newfound strength, we illustrate the idea that adversity has the power to spark positive change and personal growth.

In this chapter, we journey through the intricate landscape of the human psyche as it responds to adversity, and we discover that within the crucible of challenge lies the potential for remarkable resilience and transformation. Through a blend of scientific research and inspiring stories, we come to understand that adversity, far from being a hindrance, can be a powerful catalyst for personal growth and the development of antifragility.

Case Studies in Overcoming Adversity: Inspiring Stories of Personal Growth

In the second chapter of our journey, we're delving even deeper into the heart of antifragility. Our focus remains firmly fixed on the intriguing concept of adversity. As we navigate this fascinating terrain, we're embarking on a complex journey that uncovers the very essence of adversity and its pivotal role in shaping our lives. Think of it like a skilled sculptor meticulously chiseling away at a block of marble to reveal the magnificent form within – adversity holds the power to transform us into resilient, wise, and fortitudinous beings.

In this chapter, our attention shifts to the tangible, to the real-life experiences of individuals. We're bringing to the forefront stories that serve as vivid testaments to the incredible potential for personal growth and transformation when we confront adversity head-on. These stories aren't just accounts; they're living proof of the remarkable capacity of the human spirit to rise, evolve, and flourish even in the face of life's most daunting challenges.

Let's start by acknowledging a universal truth: adversity doesn't discriminate. It doesn't care about your age, gender, or social status. Its presence is as impartial as the rain that falls on both the virtuous and the not-so-virtuous. To illustrate this point, we'll draw upon the real-life stories of individuals who've confronted adversity head-on and emerged from the ordeal stronger and wiser. We aim to breathe life into the concept of adversity. It's not just an abstract idea; it's something many people live through. Through these case studies, we hope to show how real people have faced adversity, navigated its tumultuous waters, and emerged on the other side as more resilient, wiser individuals.

Charlotte Brown - Vaulting Beyond Limits: In the quaint town of Millican, Texas, Charlotte Brown confronted a challenge that could have easily shattered her dreams. As she entered high school, she had already lost her sight. Blindness could have appeared as an insurmountable obstacle, but Charlotte was resolute in her determination not to let it define her.

High school typically marks a period when teenagers discover their identities and passions, and for Charlotte, that passion was pole vaulting. She adamantly refused to allow her disability to hold her back. In her senior year, she achieved the seemingly impossible—she secured the bronze medal at the Texas state high school championships, competing alongside sighted athletes. The exhilarating cheers of the crowd and the sensation of soaring over the bar fueled her unwavering determination.

However, Charlotte's story didn't conclude there. She carried her dreams to Purdue University, where she continued to pole vault at the collegiate level. Her indomitable spirit and relentless pursuit of her aspirations served as an inspiration to everyone in her orbit. Charlotte Brown epitomized the notion that adversity can indeed be a steppingstone to greatness.

Inky Johnson - From Gridiron to the World Stage: Inky Johnson, originally Inquoris Desmond Chade Johnson, possessed a bright football career at the University of Tennessee, with the NFL on the horizon thanks to his talent and unwavering commitment. Yet, a single game would forever alter his course.

During a fateful tackle, Inky found himself immobilized on the field, discovering that his right arm was irrevocably paralyzed. The NFL dreams he had relentlessly pursued were instantaneously shattered.

Nevertheless, Inky Johnson was not one to succumb to adversity. He made the deliberate choice to redefine his purpose and inspire others through his remarkable story. Transforming into a motivational speaker, he embarked on a global journey, touching lives profoundly with his impactful words. In doing so, Inky illustrated that resilience extends beyond mere recovery; it's about harnessing adversity as a springboard toward unparalleled achievement.

Myron Golden - From Polio to Prosperity: Myron Golden's early years were marked by the harsh reality of contracting polio, a debilitating illness. However, he steadfastly refused to let his circumstances define him. Myron's journey from poverty and disability to prosperity and success is nothing short of remarkable.

Guided by discipline and faith, Myron used these principles as his north star. Rather than allowing his disability to limit him, he harnessed it as a driving force propelling him toward greatness. Today, he stands as a best-selling author in the field of personal finance and financial literacy, with his book "From the Trash Man to The Cash Man" transforming countless lives, including mine.

Myron's uplifting messages, deeply rooted in Biblically sound doctrine, resonate profoundly with individuals seeking financial empowerment. He has become a symbol of hope, demonstrating that adversity can indeed serve as a steppingstone to financial well-being.

Nick Vujicic - No Limbs, No Limits: Nick Vujicic's life began with an unimaginable challenge—he was born without arms and legs due to Tetra-amelia syndrome. His parents faced a moment of shock and disbelief, but Nick's determination would soon become evident.

At the age of 10, Nick reached a point of despair and attempted suicide, feeling overwhelmed by the physical challenges he faced. However, he found the strength to persevere and embarked on a journey to inspire the world.

Nick's passion for sharing his story and motivating others to appreciate their lives has taken him across the globe. He has become a hero to countless individuals, demonstrating that even with extraordinary physical challenges, one can rise above adversity and lead a fulfilling life. Nick's story is a testament to the incredible resilience of the human spirit.

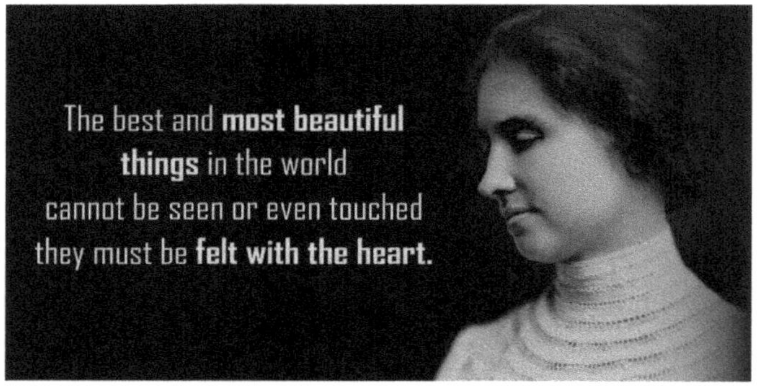

Helen Keller - Triumph Over Darkness and Silence: Helen Keller's story transcends time and continues to inspire generations. Born blind and deaf in the late 19th century, her circumstances were daunting. Yet, she defied the odds and accomplished extraordinary educational, advocacy, and writing accomplishments.

Despite living in an era without advanced medical treatments, Helen Keller's determination knew no bounds. She became the first deaf-blind person to earn a bachelor's degree, authored the famous autobiography "The Story of My Life," and travelled as a lecturer, advocating for people with disabilities.

Helen Keller's support for women's rights, pacifism, and civil rights made her a prominent humanitarian and co-founder of the American Civil Liberties Union. Her life story is a timeless example of resilience and the boundless potential of the human spirit, inspiring countless individuals to overcome their own challenges and positively impact the world.

These case studies offer concrete examples of how individuals can rise above adversity, embracing it as an opportunity for personal growth and transformation. Through their stories, we witness the incredible resilience of the human spirit and gain valuable insights into the practical application of antifragility principles in our own lives.

As we venture further into this chapter, we delve into the intriguing realm of psychological research. Our aim is to uncover the science that explains why adversity, paradoxically, can serve as a catalyst for positive change. This phenomenon is often referred to as "post-traumatic growth," a process through which individuals, in the aftermath of adversity, experience personal development and newfound strength.

We explore how adversity can function as a vessel for resilience, forging individuals into unbreakable spirits capable of withstanding life's tempestuous challenges. It is within these trials that we unearth hidden reservoirs of courage, adaptability, and tenacity.

However, adversity, like any potent force, can be a double-edged sword. Its impact largely depends on our perspective and response. Do we perceive it as an insurmountable obstacle, or do we recognize it as an opportunity for growth? In the chapters that lie ahead, we will uncover practical strategies for cultivating a mindset that fully embraces adversity as a catalyst for positive transformation.

As we conclude this chapter, it is essential to remember that adversity is not a malevolent force conspiring against us; rather, it is the chisel that artfully sculpts the masterpiece of our lives. It serves as the crucible that carefully refines our character and functions as the mirror that reflects our true potential. When faced with adversity, we have a choice—to wither in its shadow or to flourish in its wake. In the face of life's formidable challenges, we possess the innate capacity to ignite the unbreakable spirit within us and emerge from the receptacle of adversity as individuals imbued with strength and unwavering resilience.

CHAPTER
3
THE WISDOM
OF RESILIENCE

The Foundations of Resilience: Understanding its Core Principles

In the third chapter of our deep dive into the fascinating concept of antifragility, we're turning our focus to what's essentially the foundation of resilience. In this section, we're going to thoroughly explore the fundamental principles that underpin resilience, which are closely linked to the whole idea of antifragility.

Resilience is often defined as the ability to endure tough times and come back stronger after facing challenges. It's not a simple concept; it's made up of various essential elements. To really grasp how resilience ties in with the broader concept of antifragility, it's crucial to take a closer look at these core principles:

- **Adaptability**: We explore the inherent adaptability of resilient individuals. In the face of change and adversity, they exhibit a remarkable capacity to adjust and respond effectively. This adaptability is a key aspect of antifragility, as it enables individuals not only to endure but to thrive amid uncertainty.

- **Emotional Regulation**: Emotional resilience is a critical component. We explore how individuals with strong resilience can regulate their emotions, allowing them to process difficult experiences without being overwhelmed. This emotional control aligns with antifragility, as it empowers individuals to remain steady in the face of life's turbulence.

- **Mindset and Positivity**: Resilience is closely linked to one's mindset and capacity for positivity. Resilient individuals often possess a growth-oriented perspective, viewing challenges as opportunities for learning and development. This mindset aligns with the antifragility ethos of leveraging adversity for positive transformation.

By comprehending these core elements, we can not only enhance our resilience but also set the stage for cultivating antifragility.

Exploring Emotional Resilience and Mental Fortitude on the Path to Antifragility

Within the intricate web of life, a profound interplay unfolds between resilience and antifragility. To embark on the path to true antifragility, one must first grasp and harness the transformative power of resilience. In this chapter, we set forth on a journey through the labyrinth of human emotions and mental fortitude, meticulously unraveling the wisdom of resilience and its intricate relationship with our overarching quest to achieve antifragility.

The Tapestry of Emotions

Life, as we know it, weaves a tapestry interlaced with a myriad of emotions. From the exuberant highs of joy and success to the profound depths of sorrow and adversity, our emotional landscape is in perpetual flux. The journey toward antifragility entails recognizing and embracing the full spectrum of these emotions while concurrently nurturing the resilience to skillfully traverse their undulating terrain.

Scriptural Wisdom: "A merry heart doeth good like a medicine: but a broken spirit drieth the bones." – Proverbs 17:22 (KJV)

The age-old wisdom encapsulated within these words resonates with the profound connection between our emotional well-being and our overall vitality. A joyful heart, enriched with positivity and resilience, indeed possesses the potential to serve as a rejuvenating elixir in the presence of life's formidable challenges.

Building Emotional Resilience

How can we strengthen our emotional resilience amid the tumultuous seas of existence? The answer lies in comprehending that resilience does not entail the absence of adversity but rather the capacity to rebound from it. It's the ability to channel our emotional responses into catalysts for growth.

Scriptural Wisdom: "We are troubled on every side, yet not distressed; we are perplexed, but not in despair." – 2 Corinthians 4:8 (KJV)

These words serve as a poignant reminder that even in the face of tribulations, we can remain unbroken. It is not about evading life's storms but rather navigating them with unwavering strength. As we delve into the practical strategies for cultivating emotional resilience, it is imperative to bear in mind that it is through the furnace of adversity that the finest steel is forged.

The Citadel of Mental Fortitude

Beyond emotional resilience lies the formidable fortress of mental fortitude. It is the capacity to withstand the most turbulent intellectual storms and emerge not only unscathed but strengthened. The journey toward antifragility demands a profound transformation of our thought patterns and mental processes.

Scriptural Wisdom: "Finally, brethren, whatsoever things are true, whatsoever things are honest, whatsoever things are just, whatsoever things are pure, whatsoever things are lovely, whatsoever things are of good report; if there be any virtue, and if there be any praise, think on these things." – Philippians 4:8 (KJV)

This scripture imparts timeless wisdom by encouraging us to channel our mental energies toward the virtuous and the positive. In the context of antifragility, it serves as a reminder that our thoughts possess the power to shape our reality. By consciously directing our mental faculties toward positivity, we not only cultivate resilience but also lay the robust foundation for the edifice of antifragility.

The Path Forward

As we draw this chapter to a close, let us take a moment to contemplate the profound interplay between emotional resilience, mental fortitude, and our journey towards achieving antifragility. To attain unbreakable strength, we must wholeheartedly embrace our emotions, navigate adversity with poise and grace, and nurture a mindset that thrives in the face of life's challenges.

In the upcoming chapters, we will dive deeper into the practical strategies for constructing emotional and mental resilience.

We will embark on an exploration of the clairvoyant processes that turn adversity into strength and transform setbacks into steppingstones along our path to antifragility. As we navigate this intricate terrain, let it be a reminder that the wisdom of resilience serves as the key that unlocks the door to an indomitable spirit.

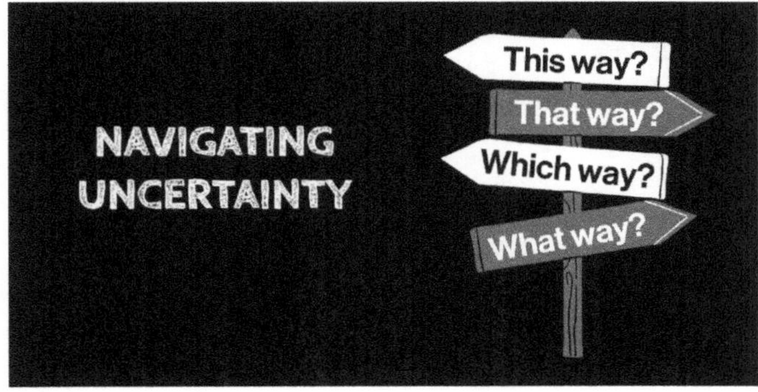

CHAPTER
4
NAVIGATING
UNCERTAINTY

The Nature of Uncertainty: Understanding its Inherent Qualities

Life has this knack for throwing curveballs at us. We've all been there, facing situations where we can't predict what will happen next. That's what this chapter is all about—dealing with life's uncertainty. We will dive into what uncertainty really is and what it means for us.

Uncertainty, at its core, is all about not knowing what's coming. It's like trying to predict the weather in a place where it changes every five minutes. You can't control it, and you can't always prepare for it. But throughout history, people have tried to make sense of this unpredictable beast.

In the past, folks like the Stoics, those ancient Greek philosophers, had some wisdom to share. They believed in accepting the things we can't control and focusing on what we can. It's kind of like the serenity prayer you might have heard—accepting what we can't change and having the courage to change what we can.

Uncertainty, though, has this interesting duality. On one side, it can be pretty scary. Not knowing can breed anxiety and fear. But on the flip side, it's also where the magic happens. Think about it; some of the most innovative and groundbreaking moments in history came from the unknown.

In today's world, uncertainty is like a constant companion. Technology is advancing at warp speed, and our lives are more interconnected than ever. Modern theories like chaos theory and the butterfly effect help us understand how small changes can lead to big outcomes. They remind us that the world is a complex, interconnected web of possibilities.

And then, there's the existential side of uncertainty. It's not just about what happens around us; it's about the big questions. Who are we? Why are we here? How do we find meaning in a world where everything is so uncertain?

Navigating Uncertainty and Building Antifragility

In the complex fabric of life, uncertainty is the unchanging thread that runs through every moment we experience. It's a constant companion, occasionally hidden in the background, and at times, making itself known without reservation. But as we begin this chapter, we embark on a journey into the deep wisdom of navigating uncertainty. We'll draw from both age-old philosophies and contemporary theories to shed light on the path that lies ahead.

Embracing the Inevitable

Uncertainty, in its many forms, is an undeniable aspect of our human journey. It weaves its way through both our personal and professional lives, carrying with it stories of change and unpredictability. The initial stride toward embracing antifragility in the presence of uncertainty is not to see it as an enemy but rather as a transformative agent.

Words of Wisdom: "For what is your life? It is even a vapour, that appeareth for a little time, and then vanisheth away." – James 4:14 (KJV)

This verse offers a poignant reflection on the fleeting nature of life itself. Uncertainty, in all its manifestations, serves as a reminder of the transient quality of our earthly existence. Recognizing this impermanence grants us a perspective that empowers us to confront uncertainty with greater courage and resilience.

The Stoic Philosophy of Equanimity

The Stoics, ancient philosophers renowned for their wisdom, extolled the virtues of equanimity or calmness in the face of uncertainty. They firmly believed that it's not the uncertainty itself but our response to it that ultimately shapes its impact. To progress toward antifragility, we must diligently cultivate the Stoic art of maintaining inner tranquility even amid the whirlwind of uncertainty.

Stoic Insight: "Man is not worried by real problems so much as by his imagined anxieties about real problems." – Epictetus

Epictetus, the Stoic philosopher, astutely recognized that our anxieties often originate not from the events themselves but from our perceptions and imagined fears surrounding them. To adeptly navigate the maze of uncertainty, it is imperative that we differentiate between genuine concerns and the illusory anxieties that tend to obscure our judgment.

The Modern Science of Resilience

Modern psychology grants us profound insight into resilience, the close kin of antifragility. Resilience embodies the ability to rebound from adversity, to endure the buffeting winds of uncertainty, and to emerge from trials even more robust. By refining our resilience, we gain the capacity to traverse the unpredictable waters of life with grace and unwavering strength.

Resilient Wisdom: "Out of difficulties grow miracles." – Jean de La Bruyère

Jean de La Bruyère's words resonate deeply with the essence of antifragility. It is within the crucible of difficulties that the seeds of our personal growth find fertile ground, and from these very challenges, miracles can indeed sprout forth.

The Path Forward

In the chapters that lie ahead, we'll delve deeper into the art of becoming antifragile, drawing inspiration from the profound wisdom of ages past and the cutting-edge insights of the present. Uncertainty, in all its diverse forms, is the very canvas upon which the masterpiece of our antifragile spirit takes shape. Embrace it, cultivate equanimity, and nurture resilience, for they are the steadfast pillars of your unyielding spirit on this transformative journey.

CHAPTER
5
ANTIFRAGILITY IN
RELATIONSHIPS

You know, relationships are kind of like a rollercoaster. They can lift us to incredible heights of joy, but they can also take us on unexpected dips into adversity. That's what this chapter is all about—how we can use the principles of antifragility to make our personal relationships even stronger and more resilient.

Think about the people in your life—friends, family, spouse, coworkers. They bring love, support, and sometimes, they bring challenges. Antifragility is about not just surviving those challenges but thriving because of them.

Imagine a relationship as a plant. It needs care, attention, and sometimes, it even needs a little pruning. But when it faces storms, it can grow deeper roots and become more resilient. That's what we aim to achieve—building bonds that can withstand life's storms and come out  even more connected. The same is true for our relationships with God. We need to be attuned to His voice and listen for what He's saying.

When we are, we can learn how to grow in love, compassion, patience, and perseverance.

Without relationships, we are alone. And without the support of others, we can do nothing. Relationships are what make us human. They are the building blocks of our existence; they give us meaning and purpose in life. Without them, we are empty shells devoid of connection and love.

In the intricate dance of human existence, relationships hold a unique place as both our most profound sources of joy and our most challenging arenas of adversity. This chapter delves into the delicate tapestry of human connections, exploring how the profound principles of antifragility can be artfully woven into the fabric of our personal and professional relationships. Our aim is not just to survive the ups and downs of these relationships but to nurture growth, resilience, and lasting connections.

The Fragile Dance of Relationships

Often, relationships are perceived as fragile, similar to delicate entities that might shatter at the slightest turbulence. Like fine porcelain, they appear susceptible to breakage under the pressures of adversity. However, the antifragile perspective invites us to challenge this notion, encouraging us to consider that relationships, akin to certain resilient materials, can actually strengthen when subjected to the right stressors.

Reflection: "A friend loveth at all times, and a brother is born for adversity." – Proverbs 17:17 (KJV)

The ancient wisdom found in Proverbs beautifully underscores the enduring nature of genuine friendship. It teaches us that authentic relationships aren't solely built during fair-weather moments but are most profoundly forged in the eruptions of adversity.

The Catalyst of Adversity

Adversity, in all its diverse forms, possesses the dual potential to either strain or strengthen relationships. It acts as the crucible through which the bonds between individuals are tested, and under the right conditions, these bonds can emerge even more robust than before. In the narratives of ordinary individuals who have harnessed the power of antifragility in their relationships, we uncover the secrets not only to enduring challenges but to thriving because of them.

The Art of Constructive Conflict

Conflict, often perceived as the nemesis of harmonious relationships, takes on a transformative dimension when viewed through the lens of antifragility. Constructive conflict, guided by mutual respect and a shared commitment to growth, can be likened to the wind that fans the flames of understanding, ultimately leading to stronger, more resilient connections.

Guiding Principle: "In the multitude of counsellors there is safety." – Proverbs 11:14 (KJV)

Proverbs wisely remind us of the value in seeking counsel and engaging in dialogue with those we hold dear. It is through these thoughtful conversations that we harness the power of constructive conflict, fostering greater understanding and deeper connections.

Professional Relationships and Growth

Beyond the realm of personal connections, antifragility extends its reach to professional relationships. The workplace, often marked by its unique challenges and competitive dynamics, can indeed transform into fertile ground for growth and collaboration when infused with antifragile principles.

Practical Wisdom: "Two are better than one; because they have a good reward for their labour." – Ecclesiastes 4:9 (KJV)

Ecclesiastes underscores the inherent value of collaboration and partnership in the pursuit of shared goals. In professional relationships, the synergy between individuals can serve as the driving force behind innovation and the catalyst for achieving success.

The Path Ahead

As we navigate the diverse landscapes of our relationships, it's crucial to remember that they need not be perceived as fragile, brittle constructs easily threatened by adversity. Instead, they can and should be antifragile. In the crucible of challenges, bonds can strengthen, love can deepen, and understanding can flourish. This chapter serves as a testament to the transformative power of applying antifragility to the realm of relationships, shedding light on the path toward growth, connection, and enduring resilience.

CHAPTER
6
THRIVING IN
CAREER AND BUSINESS

Antifragility extends to the professional realm, where individuals and organizations alike can harness the power of embracing challenges to achieve lasting success and foster innovation. In this chapter, we delve into the concept of antifragility as it relates to the world of work, exploring how it can be a guiding principle for personal and professional development.

Personal Antifragility in Career Growth: Navigating Challenges for Professional Development

In the ever-evolving landscape of the modern workplace, the ability to adapt and thrive amidst uncertainty and adversity has become paramount. This concept of personal antifragility in career growth revolves around the idea that individuals can not only withstand challenges but actually grow stronger when exposed to them.

Embracing Challenges: To truly thrive in one's career, it is essential to embrace challenges as opportunities for growth rather than viewing them as obstacles. Challenges can take many forms, from job-related hurdles to industry-wide disruptions. Instead of fearing these challenges, individuals can cultivate a mindset that welcomes them as a chance to learn, adapt, and ultimately excel.

Continuous Learning: Personal antifragility in career growth hinges on the willingness to engage in continuous learning. The most successful professionals are those who actively seek out new knowledge and skills, even when they are not required to do so. This approach not only enhances one's capabilities but also positions them to navigate unforeseen challenges with confidence.

Resilience in the Face of Setbacks: Setbacks are an inevitable part of any career journey. However, those who are personally antifragile use setbacks as steppingstones rather than stumbling blocks. They learn from failures, adapt their strategies, and come back stronger. Resilience, therefore, becomes a key attribute in the pursuit of career growth.

Networking and Collaboration: Antifragility extends beyond individual growth; it also encompasses the ability to forge connections and collaborate with others. Building a strong professional network and seeking out opportunities for collaboration can provide a support system that helps individuals navigate challenges more effectively.

Innovation and Creativity: Embracing antifragility in career growth encourages individuals to think innovatively and creatively. When faced with challenges, they are more likely to find unique solutions and drive innovation within their organizations. This innovative spirit can lead to breakthroughs and position individuals as valuable assets in their respective fields.

Balancing Risk and Reward: Personal antifragility in career growth requires a careful balance between taking risks and assessing potential rewards. While it is essential to take calculated risks to propel one's career forward, it is equally important to weigh the potential benefits against the possible downsides.

Thriving in the Business Arena: The Power of Antifragility in Professional Life.

In the fast-paced world of careers and business, where challenges and opportunities go hand in hand, antifragility becomes a valuable ally. This chapter is like a guided tour through the ever-changing landscapes of professional life. It reveals the strategies and perspectives that empower both individuals and organizations not only to withstand the inevitable challenges but to thrive and find new opportunities within them.

The Ever-Changing Business Landscape

The business world, as we know it, is an arena filled with uncertainties. Economic tides rise and fall, markets shift like shifting sands, and technological waves keep rolling in. However, the antifragile perspective encourages us not to view these challenges as threats, but rather as steppingstones toward greater innovation and success.

Here's a guiding principle to consider: "For which of you, intending to build a tower, sitteth not down first, and counteth the cost, whether he have sufficient to finish it?" — Luke 14:28 (KJV)

The wisdom found in Luke's words teaches us a valuable lesson about the importance of careful planning and foresight in the world of business. Antifragility isn't synonymous with recklessness; it's about taking calculated risks and making well-informed decisions.

Innovating Through Adversity

Challenges in the realm of business frequently act as catalysts for innovation. By embracing an antifragile perspective, both individuals and organizations can harness adversity's energy to ignite creativity and propel progress. The stories of pioneering companies and entrepreneurs who transformed setbacks into springboards for innovation motivate us to perceive obstacles not as roadblocks but as steppingstones to growth.

Here's a piece of practical wisdom to consider: "And the Lord said unto Moses, wherefore criest thou unto me? speak unto the children of Israel, that they go forward." — Exodus 14:15 (KJV)

The book of Exodus offers a profound reminder that even when confronted with what appears to be insurmountable challenges, progress can be achieved by taking one step forward. In the world of business, just as in life, moving ahead, no matter how small the stride, can lead to extraordinary outcomes.

Welcoming Change

The capacity to welcome change is a defining trait of antifragility within the professional domain. Within these pages, we'll delve into the strategies and mindsets that enable both individuals and organizations not only to navigate change effectively but also to harness it as a powerful catalyst for growth and innovation.

Consider this reflection: "To every thing there is a season, and a time to every purpose under the heaven." – Ecclesiastes 3:1 (KJV)

The Book of Ecclesiastes imparts the wisdom of seasons, serving as a poignant reminder that change is an intrinsic part of life. In our careers and businesses, recognizing and adapting to the seasons of change can lead to enduring and sustainable success.

The Unending Journey

As you embark on the intricate journey of thriving in your career and business endeavors, always remember that antifragility is not a final destination but an ongoing expedition. It encompasses a mindset, a set of strategies, and an unwavering belief that even when adversity rears its head, success remains not only attainable but can even be enhanced. This chapter serves as your trusted guide through the dynamic landscapes of professional life, offering invaluable insights and inspiration to help you navigate challenges, ignite innovation, and emerge stronger on your path to lasting success.

In conclusion, achieving personal antifragility in career growth entails cultivating the mindset and honing the skills necessary to thrive when faced with obstacles. By perceiving adversity as an opportunity for personal development, fostering a commitment to continuous learning, and building resilience, individuals can skillfully navigate the ever-changing professional terrain. This proactive approach not only benefits individuals but also contributes to the overall antifragility of organizations and entire industries.

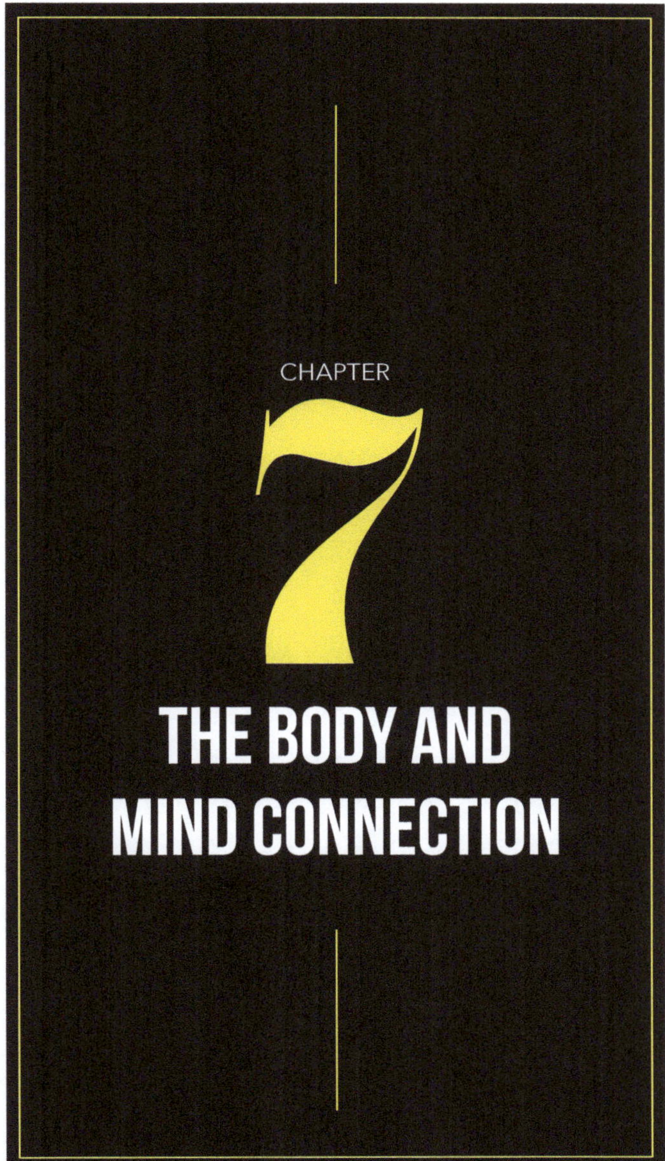
CHAPTER
7
THE BODY AND
MIND CONNECTION

In the intricate dance of life, the connection between our physical well-being and mental fortitude is a profound testament to the principles of antifragility. This chapter delves into the harmony between our bodies and minds, revealing how they intertwine to create a resilient foundation even in the face of life's most daunting challenges.

The Role of Exercise and Nutrition in Antifragility.

Nourishing the Body: Our bodies are the vessels that carry us through life's trials and tribulations. To become antifragile, we must nurture and fortify this vessel. Exercise and nutrition stand as the cornerstone of this endeavor.

Regular physical activity not only strengthens our muscles but also enhances our resilience. It is through the stress and recovery cycles of exercise that our bodies adapt and grow stronger, mirroring the principles of antifragility.

Exercise for the Mind: The mind, too, requires exercise of a different kind.

Mental resilience is a critical component of antifragility. We will delve into mindfulness practices and stress management techniques that nurture our mental fortitude.

Through mindfulness, we learn to embrace the present moment and develop the capacity to respond to life's challenges with clarity and composure. Stress management equips us with the tools to navigate adversity without succumbing to its detrimental effects.

Mindfulness and Stress Management for Mental Resilience

In the hustle and bustle of modern life, where stress and uncertainty often loom large, the practice of mindfulness emerges as a powerful tool to bolster mental resilience. Mindfulness is not merely a trendy buzzword but a timeless practice that allows individuals to remain grounded, centered, and emotionally agile in the face of adversity.

Scriptural Wisdom: "Be still, and know that I am God." – Psalm 46:10 (KJV)

The wisdom encapsulated in this scripture underscores the importance of stillness and self-awareness. In the context of antifragility, it reminds us that in the stillness of mindfulness, we find clarity, inner strength, and the capacity to navigate life's challenges with poise.

Mindfulness is the art of being present in the moment, fully aware of our thoughts, emotions, and sensations. By cultivating this practice, individuals can develop a heightened sense of self-awareness, allowing them to respond to stressors with a calm and measured demeanor. Rather than reacting impulsively, they gain the ability to assess situations with greater clarity and make well-informed decisions.

Stress, a ubiquitous companion in our lives, can either shatter our mental resilience or serve as a catalyst for growth, depending on how we perceive and manage it. Mindfulness equips us with the tools to transform stress from a debilitating force into a source of personal development.

Through mindfulness, individuals learn to acknowledge their stressors without judgment, allowing them to explore the underlying causes of their reactions. This self-awareness empowers them to address stress at its root, fostering a more adaptive and resilient mindset.

Moreover, mindfulness practices often incorporate relaxation techniques such as deep breathing and meditation. These techniques can help individuals manage stress physiologically by lowering heart rate, reducing blood pressure, and promoting a sense of calm. By integrating these practices into their daily routines, individuals can enhance their mental resilience and emotional well-being.

In conclusion, the practice of mindfulness and stress management is an essential component of cultivating mental resilience in the context of antifragility. It empowers individuals to harness the power of the mind, fostering inner strength, adaptability, and a capacity to thrive even in the face of life's trials.

The Body's Resilience

The human body, a marvel of complexity, possesses an inherent antifragility. It is designed to adapt, grow, and heal through challenges. Our muscles become stronger with exercise, our bones denser with weight-bearing stress, and our immune systems more robust when exposed to pathogens. These physical adaptations showcase the body's capacity to not only endure but to thrive under pressure.

Profound Insight: "Know ye not that ye are the temple of God, and that the Spirit of God dwelleth in you?" – 1 Corinthians 3:16 (KJV)

1 Corinthians reminds us of the sanctity of our bodies. Caring for our physical temple is an act of reverence, and in doing so, we harness our inherent antifragility.

The Mind's Resilience

The human mind, a fortress of consciousness, is equally endowed with antifragility. It thrives when challenged, adapting, and evolving to conquer adversity. Resilience of the mind enables us to face life's uncertainties with clarity and courage. Through stories of individuals who have triumphed over mental trials, we've already unveiled the potential of the human mind to not only endure but to flourish amid adversity.

The Symbiotic Dance

The intricate connection between the body and mind creates a symbiotic dance, were physical health bolsters mental resilience and vice versa. This chapter explores practical strategies to nurture this connection, from exercise and nutrition to mindfulness and meditation. By adopting a holistic approach to well-being, we can unlock our antifragile potential.

Guiding Principle: "And be not conformed to this world: but be ye transformed by the renewing of your mind." – Romans 12:2 (KJV)

Romans teaches us the transformative power of renewing our minds. It is in this renewal that we discover our antifragile capacity to thrive amidst the tumultuous currents of life.

Cultivating Antifragility

As you embark on the path to embracing antifragility within your body and mind, remember that this journey is not about perfection but progress. It's about recognizing the profound connection between your physical well-being and mental fortitude and nurturing this connection with care and intention. By doing so, you will not only endure the storms of life but emerge from them stronger, more resilient, and unbreakable, a living testament to the unrelenting human spirit.

CHAPTER
8
CULTIVATING
ANTIFRAGILE HABITS

In the pursuit of antifragility, the development of specific habits and practices assumes a critical role. This chapter delves into the realm of daily rituals that, although seemingly small, possess immense transformative power. These rituals serve as the bedrock of resilience and adaptability, nurturing the qualities essential for thriving in the face of adversity.

As we embark on the path to becoming antifragile, we arrive at a pivotal juncture where our habits and practices wield transformative influence. This chapter stands as our practical guide, offering insights into the cultivation of habits that amplify resilience and adaptability. It empowers us to not only withstand life's challenges but to flourish amid them.

The Daily Rituals of Resilience: Small Practices with Big Impact"

In the grand tapestry of life, it's often the daily threads that weave the most significant patterns. This part unveils the small yet potent practices that can fortify our resilience on a day-to-day basis. From morning routines that set the tone for the day to evening rituals that promote restful sleep, these daily habits are the keystones of antifragility.

We will delve into practices such as mindfulness meditation, gratitude journaling, and physical exercise. These seemingly straightforward actions, when consistently integrated into your life, can have a profound impact on your ability to endure challenges and emerge stronger.

In the sphere of personal growth and resilience, simple yet potent practices can yield remarkable results. Let's explore three of these transformative habits:

1. **Mindfulness Meditation:** This ancient practice involves focusing your attention on the present moment, observing your thoughts and sensations without judgment. Mindfulness meditation has been scientifically proven to reduce stress, increase emotional regulation, and enhance overall mental well-being. By regularly engaging in mindfulness meditation, you sharpen your ability to remain calm and centered, even in

the midst of life's storms. It allows you to detach from the chaos of external challenges and find inner peace, a key ingredient in antifragility.

2. **Gratitude Journaling:** The act of expressing gratitude for the positive aspects of your life through journaling can foster a resilient mindset. By routinely reflecting on the things you're thankful for, you shift your focus from what you lack to what you have. This shift in perspective enhances your mental resilience and helps you maintain a positive outlook, making you more adept at navigating adversities.

3. **Physical Exercise:** Regular physical activity is not only beneficial for your body but also for your mind. Exercise releases endorphins, the body's natural mood elevators, and reduces stress hormones. Engaging in physical exercise not only strengthens your body but also fortifies your mental resilience. It boosts your confidence,

reduces anxiety, and increases your capacity to face challenges head-on. Physical fitness is a cornerstone of antifragility, as a healthy body forms the basis for a resilient mind.

While these practices may seem simple, their cumulative impact is profound. Incorporating mindfulness meditation, gratitude journaling, and regular physical exercise into your daily life can build the emotional and mental resilience needed to thrive amidst adversity. These habits serve as pillars of strength, enabling you to withstand challenges and emerge from them even stronger, a true testament to the power of antifragility.

By focusing on the rituals that enhance your mental and emotional well-being, you can navigate life's uncertainties with greater clarity, calmness, and inner strength. The daily rituals of resilience, examined in this section, are your toolkit for cultivating antifragility one day at a time.

Harnessing the Power of Antifragile Habits for Personal Growth and Resilience

Embracing antifragile habits is a gateway to personal growth and resilience. These habits, when integrated into your daily life, act as anchors in the face of adversity, allowing you to not only endure but thrive. By cultivating practices that enhance your adaptability and fortitude, you unlock the potential to become a more resilient, unbreakable version of yourself.

The Power of Habits

Habits, those seemingly small routines woven into the fabric of our daily lives, possess astonishing power. They can either propel us forward or hold us back. In the quest for antifragility, recognizing the influence of habits is paramount. Drawing inspiration from those who have harnessed the potency of habits to transform their lives, we uncover the blueprint for cultivating our own.

Insightful Wisdom: "Sow a thought, and you reap an act; sow an act, and you reap a habit; sow a habit, and you reap a character;

sow a character, and you reap a destiny." – Samuel Smiles

Samuel Smiles reminds us that our destiny is intricately linked to our habits. By sowing the right thoughts and acts, we can cultivate habits that lead us toward becoming antifragile.

The Habits of Antifragility

In this part, we dive deep into the habits and practices that exemplify antifragility. From the power of embracing discomfort and seeking continuous learning to the resilience forged through adversity, we unearth the key habits that propel individuals toward thriving, not just surviving, amidst life's challenges.

The Antifragile Mindset

At the heart of cultivating antifragile habits lies a mindset that welcomes challenges as opportunities. We delve into the concept of a growth mindset and its role in strengthening our ability to adapt, learn, and evolve. By adopting this mindset, we become architects of our own antifragility.

Foundational Principle: "For as he thinketh in his heart, so is he." – Proverbs 23:7

Proverbs remind us that our thoughts shape our reality. By embracing a growth mindset, we mold ourselves into individuals capable of thriving through adversity.

Practical Strategies

This chapter provides you with practical strategies for incorporating antifragile habits into your daily life. From setting intentional goals and monitoring your progress to establishing a nurturing environment for growth, you will uncover actionable steps to nurture resilience and adaptability.

Guiding Light: "The journey of a thousand miles begins with one step." – Lao Tzu Lao

Tzu's wisdom reminds us that transformation begins with a single step. Every habit you cultivate serves as a building block in the construction of your antifragile journey.

Your Antifragile Path

As you embark on this chapter, keep in mind that the development of antifragile habits is an ongoing journey rather than a final destination. It's about making progress, not achieving perfection. By embracing these practices, you empower yourself not only to withstand life's challenges but to emerge from them with greater strength, resilience, and unshakable determination. Your path towards antifragility serves as a testament to the enduring human spirit, a shining beacon of hope that adversity marks not the end, but the beginning of your boundless potential.

CHAPTER
9
THE POWER
OF MINDSET

In the grand tapestry of becoming antifragile, few threads are as essential as the one we weave with our mindset. This chapter delves into the profound influence of our mental attitudes and introduces you to the concept of a growth mindset, a powerful tool that aligns seamlessly with the journey of embracing antifragility.

The Mindset-Resilience Connection

In the intricate tapestry of human experience, the relationship between mindset and resilience is a thread of profound significance. Our mindset, the lens through which we perceive and respond to the world, plays a pivotal role in determining our capacity to weather life's storms and emerge stronger from adversity.

Imagine your mind as the captain of a ship navigating the tempestuous seas of life. A fragile mindset quivers at the first sign of a storm, quickly succumbing to fear and uncertainty. In contrast, a resilient mindset steers the ship with confidence, adapting to the challenges that arise and charting a course toward calmer waters.

Now, consider the concept of an antifragile mindset—an approach that not only endures the tempestuous seas but thrives in their midst. This mindset not only embraces adversity as an opportunity for growth but actively seeks it out. It's the mindset that views challenges as steppingstones to greater strength and wisdom.

Sea of Possibilities: "Your mind is like this water, my friend. When it is agitated, it becomes difficult to see. But if you allow it to settle, the answer becomes clear." – Master Oogway, Kung Fu Panda

Master Oogway's wisdom, as quoted in Kung Fu Panda, reminds us of the potential for clarity that arises from a calm and settled mind. Antifragility thrives in such clarity, where we can not only endure adversity but also find the answers and opportunities hidden within its challenges.

The Growth Mindset Unveiled

At the heart of this chapter lies the growth mindset. This mindset, introduced by psychologist Carol Dweck, lies at the heart of personal development and resilience. It's the belief that our abilities and intelligence are not fixed traits but can be nurtured and expanded through dedication, learning, and effort.

Dweck's Insight:

Carol Dweck succinctly captures the essence of the growth mindset with her insightful words, "Becoming is better than being."– Carol Dweck, "Mindset: The New Psychology of Success."

In those five simple words, Dweck beautifully captures the core essence of a growth mindset: it's all about the journey of becoming, rather than fixating on a static state of being. As you delve deeper into this chapter and gain a comprehensive understanding of the principles and practices that form the bedrock of the growth mindset, you'll unlock its potential as a potent tool in your quest to become more adaptable, resilient, and, ultimately, antifragile.

Embracing Challenges as Opportunities

Antifragile individuals possess a unique perspective on challenges - they see them as opportunities for growth and transformation. Unlike those who might instinctively avoid difficulties or become overwhelmed by them, antifragile individuals embrace these challenges as essential components of their journey towards self-improvement and resilience.

Melanie Perkins - Designing Resilience: Melanie Perkins, the co-founder of Canva, embarked on a journey that would revolutionize the world of graphic design. Her story is a testament to the power of determination and innovation in the face of adversity.

Melanie's background as a graphic design tutor gave her a unique perspective on the challenges faced by students and professionals alike. She recognized the struggle many encountered when attempting to master complex design software like Adobe Photoshop. This recognition would become the spark for a groundbreaking idea.

The idea was Canva, a platform aimed at making graphic design easy and accessible for everyone, regardless of their level of expertise. Melanie's vision was clear, but the path to realizing it was far from smooth. She encountered numerous rejections from investors who couldn't see the potential in her concept. Countless "no's" could have easily deterred many aspiring entrepreneurs, but Melanie was not one to back down.

In the face of adversity and rejection, Melanie persevered. She believed in the transformative potential of Canva and was determined to see her dream through to fruition. Her unwavering commitment and resilience paid off, as she transformed her small idea into one of the biggest design platforms in the world.

Today, Canva is used by millions of people globally, changing the way design is approached and executed. Melanie's journey is an inspiration not only to entrepreneurs but especially to women entrepreneurs worldwide. Her story is a reminder that adversity can be the driving force behind innovation and success. Melanie Perkins turned her challenges into opportunities, proving that with determination and a clear vision, one can achieve greatness and leave a lasting impact on an industry.

Cultivating a Growth Mindset

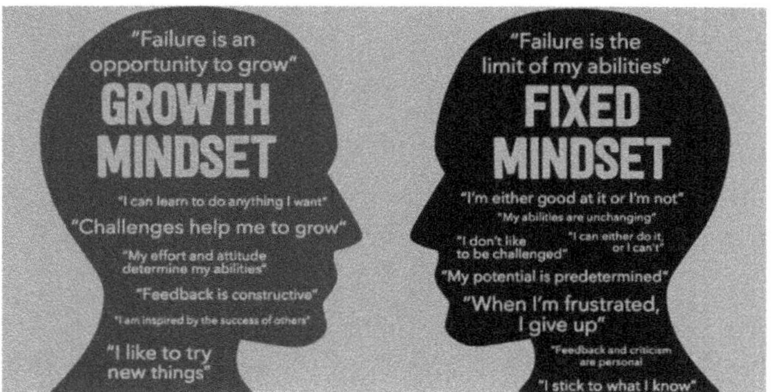

This chapter provides you with practical strategies to cultivate a growth mindset in your own life. From the power of yet ("I can't do it yet") to the magic of self-compassion, you'll discover actionable steps to nurture a mindset that thrives on adversity.

Mahatma Gandhi's quote, "Your beliefs become your thoughts, your thoughts become your words, your words become your actions, your actions become your habits, your habits become your values, your values become your destiny," is a profound reflection on the power of our beliefs to shape the course of our lives.

This quote reminds us that our beliefs are the seeds from which everything else grows. It all starts with what we believe to be true about ourselves, others, and the world around us. These beliefs then influence our thoughts, which, in turn, shape our words and actions. Over time, these actions become habits, and our repeated habits form the bedrock of our values. Ultimately, our values dictate our destiny, determining the path our lives will take.

In the context of cultivating a growth mindset, this quote underscores the importance of nurturing positive and empowering beliefs about our abilities, our capacity to learn and grow, and our potential to thrive even in the face of adversity. By consciously shaping our beliefs to align with a growth mindset, we can set in motion a chain of positive thoughts, actions, habits, values, and, ultimately, a destiny that is marked by resilience, adaptability, and the pursuit of antifragility.

The Key to Unbreakable Spirit

An unbreakable spirit is like a mental and emotional superpower that empowers someone to confront challenges head-on with unwavering determination. It's about recognizing tough situations but refusing to let them crush your resolve or dampen your inner strength.

Having an unbreakable spirit means you're resilient and flexible. You can bounce back from setbacks and failures, using them as steppingstones for personal growth and learning. Instead of giving in to despair or hopelessness, those with an unbreakable spirit summon the inner fortitude to persevere, persist, and pursue their dreams.

Importantly, having an unbreakable spirit doesn't mean you're impervious to pain or life's difficulties. It's about acknowledging those challenges, allowing yourself to feel them, but ultimately deciding not to let them define you or defeat your spirit. It's discovering that inner reservoir of strength and determination that keeps you going despite the obstacles in your path.

An unbreakable spirit serves as a powerful source of inspiration and motivation for others. It shines as a guiding light, demonstrating that triumphing over adversity and achieving success is within reach. It showcases the incredible human capacity to adapt, grow, and transform.

In essence, an unbreakable spirit is a mindset and attitude that empowers individuals to confront challenges with resilience, determination, and adaptability. It's not about being unaffected by pain or hardships but about learning from those experiences. It stands as a beacon of hope and motivation for others on their journey to overcome obstacles and lead fulfilling lives.

CHAPTER
10
ANTIFRAGILE
LEADERSHIP

In the intricate tapestry of antifragility, leadership emerges as a vital thread, weaving its influence not only through an individual's journey but also across entire teams and organizations. As we embark on this chapter's journey, we delve into the profound concept of antifragile leadership and how it acts as a guiding beacon for those who dare to navigate their teams through the turbulent seas of uncertainty.

The Traits of Antifragile Leadership: Characteristics That Foster Resilience and Innovation.

Leadership, in its essence, is about guiding a team or organization through the ever-changing currents of the professional world. In the pursuit of antifragility, leaders play a pivotal role in shaping not just the destiny of their teams but also the resilience and innovation they bring to the table.

From adaptability and a growth mindset to effective communication and the encouragement of continuous learning, antifragile leaders exemplify these characteristics, inspiring their teams to thrive amidst uncertainty and adversity.

As we embark on the journey of understanding antifragile leadership, we dive deep into the core characteristics that empower leaders to cultivate resilience and innovation within their teams. These characteristics serve as a guiding compass, illuminating the path to creating an environment where challenges cease to be perceived as threats but rather as fertile ground for growth and advancement.

Antifragile leadership isn't merely about steering a team through calm waters; it's about preparing them to navigate the storms and emerge stronger. These traits are the building blocks of leadership that thrives amidst adversity:

- **Adaptability**: Antifragile leaders possess the ability to adapt swiftly to changing circumstances. They are not rigid but flexible, embracing shifts and uncertainties with a readiness to pivot when necessary.

- **Growth Mindset**: Leaders with a growth mindset believe in the potential for development and improvement, both in themselves and their team members. They see challenges as opportunities to learn and evolve.

- **Effective Communication**: Clear and open communication is essential for antifragile leadership. Leaders must convey their vision, expectations, and support effectively, ensuring that the team remains aligned and informed.

- **Continuous Learning**: Antifragile leaders are lifelong learners, setting an example by actively seeking knowledge and encouraging their teams to do the same. They understand that learning is an ongoing process.

- **Resilience**: Leaders must model resilience, showing that setbacks are not defeats but steppingstones towards improvement. Their ability to bounce back from adversity inspires their teams to do the same.

- **Empathy and Compassion**: A deep understanding of team members' needs, concerns, and emotions is crucial. Antifragile leaders cultivate empathy and offer support, fostering a sense of belonging and trust within their teams.

- **Risk-Taking**: These leaders are not averse to calculated risks. They encourage creative thinking and innovation, allowing team members to explore new avenues and experiment without fear of failure.

- **Strategic Vision**: Antifragile leadership is not just about reacting to challenges; it's about having a long-term vision and strategy. Leaders provide a clear direction for their teams to navigate the uncertain terrain ahead.

Leadership in the Storm

Imagine a ship at sea, its crew facing a storm that threatens to engulf them. Fragile leadership would cower in the face of this turmoil, paralyzed by fear and indecision. Resilient leadership would navigate the ship through the storm, ensuring its survival. But antifragile leadership transcends this; it doesn't just weather the storm; it thrives within it.

The concept of the antifragile leader can be likened to the captain of a ship navigating through the stormy seas of adversity. Unlike fragile leaders who may retreat or crumble in the face of challenges, or even resilient leaders who aim to maintain the status quo, the antifragile leader takes a unique approach.

This leader doesn't just weather the storm; they see it as an opportunity for growth and innovation. When confronted with adversity, they don't retreat but rather steer their team or organization boldly into the storm. They understand that within chaos and turbulence lies the potential for transformation and progress.

In essence, the antifragile leader seizes adversity as a chance to learn, adapt, and become stronger. They view challenges not as obstacles but as bridges towards achieving greater resilience and success. This mindset allows them to navigate through uncertainty with confidence, using every setback as a springboard for growth and innovation, ultimately leading their team or organization to thrive amidst adversity.

Antifragile Organizations

Just as a single individual can become antifragile, so too can an organization. This chapter explores how leaders can infuse the principles of antifragility into the very DNA of their teams and companies. We'll journey through stories of remarkable organizations that have not only survived crises but emerged from them stronger and more resilient than ever.

"The Phoenix Rises" is a powerful narrative of a tech startup that exemplifies the essence of antifragile leadership. In the face of significant challenges and adversity, this organization didn't merely survive; it

thrived and transformed itself into a global powerhouse. This story serves as an inspiring example of how antifragile leadership can empower organizations to harness the forces of change and adversity to their advantage.

This particular tech startup faced a myriad of obstacles, from financial difficulties to technological disruptions and fierce competition. Rather than succumbing to these challenges or merely surviving, the leadership team adopted an antifragile mindset. They recognized that every setback was an opportunity for growth and innovation. Instead of viewing adversity as a threat, they saw it as a catalyst for positive change.

The organization embraced change and uncertainty as a way to reinvent itself continually. They encouraged experimentation, learning from failures, and adapting quickly to evolving market conditions. This agile approach allowed them to stay ahead of the curve and remain relevant in their industry.

As a result, this once-struggling tech startup not only survived but flourished. They emerged from each challenge stronger, more innovative, and better equipped to navigate an ever-changing business landscape. The story of this organization illustrates how antifragile leadership can drive lasting success and resilience at an organizational level, proving that adversity can indeed be the fertile ground from which greatness arises.

Inspiring Resilience

Antifragile leadership isn't about being an unbreakable superhero; it's about inspiring resilience in others. As we close this chapter, we delve into practical strategies that leaders can employ to cultivate an environment where individuals and teams draw strength from adversity.

Guiding Your Team

Within these pages, you'll discover invaluable guidance on how to lead by example, foster innovation, and cultivate a culture where mistakes are seen as steppingstones to growth. At the heart of antifragile leadership is the ability to embrace uncertainty and inspire your team to do the same.

The Antifragile Pledge encapsulates this ethos: "We do not fear the storm. We harness its power to sail to new horizons." This powerful pledge embodies the spirit of antifragile leadership, where challenges are not obstacles but opportunities to chart new courses and achieve remarkable success.

Antifragility as a Legacy

As a leader, the legacy you leave behind is not solely measured by the successes you attain, but by the resilient spirit you instill within your team. Embracing the role of an antifragile leader means leaving a legacy characterized by strength, adaptability, and unwavering courage.

Simon Sinek's wisdom, encapsulated in the quote "Leadership is not about being in charge. It's about taking care of those in your charge," serves as a profound reminder of what true leadership entails. It emphasizes that leadership isn't merely about holding a position of authority; it's a commitment to the well-being, growth, and development of those under your guidance. Your legacy, as an antifragile leader, lies in fostering an unbroken chain of resilience, where each link is fortified with the strength to thrive in the face of adversity.

The Call to Antifragile Leadership

As you dive into the rich concepts and inspiring stories within this chapter, it's essential to remember that antifragile leadership is not an exclusive realm for a select few; it's a universal call to action for all those who aspire to lead. It extends an open invitation to navigate the unpredictable waters of uncertainty, not with fear or hesitation, but with an unwavering spirit of resilience.

Antifragile leadership is more than just a personal journey; it's a path that beckons others to join in. It's a call to inspire those around you to become antifragile, to rise above challenges, and to thrive amidst adversity. It's a beacon of hope and a guiding light, showing the way toward unlocking the boundless potential that resides within each of us. In embracing antifragile leadership, you not only become a leader but also a catalyst for positive change, illuminating the path toward our collective greatest potential.

CHAPTER
11
EMBRACING CHANGE

Change is an inevitable and constant force in the world. Whether we like it or not, it sweeps through our personal lives and permeates the organizations we belong to. While change can be daunting, an antifragile perspective offers a powerful framework for not only adapting to change but thriving because of it. In this chapter, we delve into the realm of organizational change and explore how embracing antifragility can lead to transformation, growth, and enduring success.

Organizations, like living organisms, must evolve to survive. In a rapidly changing world, those that resist, or fear change are at risk of becoming obsolete. On the other hand, organizations that embrace change with an antifragile mindset view it as an opportunity to grow, innovate, and gain a competitive edge.

In the ever-turning pages of our lives, one thing is certain: change. It sweeps through our existence like a persistent wind, sometimes a gentle breeze, at other times a raging storm. Yet, within the heart of this constant, there lies an extraordinary power—an ability to not only adapt but to thrive amid the ebb and flow of life's transitions.

The Nature of Change

Change is the heartbeat of existence. From the changing seasons to the evolution of technology, from the transformation of our bodies to the shifting landscapes of our careers, it's a force that never ceases. Instead of resisting it, why not harness its momentum to propel us forward?

Embracing Change

Change is the heartbeat of life, a constant and dynamic force that shapes our experiences. It's woven into the fabric of our existence, from the changing seasons that mark the passage of time to the ever-evolving technology that reshapes our daily routines. Our own bodies undergo continuous change, from infancy to old age, adapting to the demands of each life stage.

Similarly, our careers and professional landscapes are in a state of constant flux, responding to economic shifts, technological advancements, and global trends.

Instead of resisting change, we can choose to embrace it as an inherent part of life. Change is not a disruption; it's the very essence of growth and progress. By understanding the nature of change and learning to navigate its currents, we can harness its momentum to propel ourselves forward.

Imagine change as the heartbeat of existence, a rhythmic and vital force that sustains life. Just as our hearts beat to circulate blood and oxygen throughout our bodies, change circulates new opportunities, experiences, and challenges into our lives. It's a force that keeps us engaged, learning, and evolving.

For example, consider the changing seasons. Each transition from winter to spring, spring to summer, and so on, brings new beauty, challenges, and experiences. Spring may bring the joy of blooming flowers and longer daylight hours, but it also presents the challenge of allergies for some. Summer may offer the pleasures of vacations and outdoor activities, but it can also bring scorching heatwaves. These seasonal changes not only provide variety but also offer opportunities for adaptation and growth.

In the realm of technology, consider how smartphones have revolutionized the way we communicate and access information. Embracing these technological changes has expanded our capabilities and connectivity, allowing us to adapt to new modes of interaction and access to knowledge.

Our bodies, too, are in a perpetual state of change. From infancy to adolescence, adulthood to old age, our physical and cognitive abilities evolve. While aging may bring challenges, such as declining physical strength or memory, it also offers the wisdom and experience that come with time.

In the professional sphere, the nature of work is continually evolving. Advances in automation, artificial intelligence, and remote work have reshaped industries and job roles. Instead of viewing these changes as threats, we can choose to see them as opportunities to acquire new skills, explore different career paths, or even create innovative solutions.

Ultimately, the nature of change is neither positive nor negative; it simply is. It's how we perceive and respond to change that determines its impact on our lives. Embracing change as a natural and inevitable part of existence allows us to harness its momentum for personal and professional growth. Just as a surfer rides the waves, we can ride the currents of change to propel ourselves forward, adapt to new challenges, and flourish in an ever-evolving world.

The Butterfly's Metamorphosis: Like the caterpillar that emerges as a butterfly, embracing change often leads to beautiful transformations. We'll explore how one individual's embrace of a career change led to a life filled with passion and purpose.

Imagine a caterpillar slowly inching its way along the ground, consumed with its daily routine and seemingly limited perspective. For much of its life, it remains confined to the familiar world of leaves and branches, focused on survival and sustenance. However, deep within this unassuming creature lies the potential for profound transformation.

At a certain point in its life cycle, the caterpillar undergoes a remarkable metamorphosis. It retreats into a chrysalis, where its body undergoes a radical transformation. Tissues break down, cells divide, and the once-crawling creature emerges as a beautiful butterfly, ready to take flight and explore new horizons.

This transformation from caterpillar to butterfly is a powerful metaphor for the potential within all of us to embrace change and undergo profound personal growth. Just as the caterpillar's life is forever altered by its metamorphosis, individuals who embrace change often find themselves on a journey of beautiful transformation, unlocking new passions and purposes.

In the realm of career change, one individual's story serves as a shining example of the Butterfly's Metamorphosis. This person, like the caterpillar, once followed a conventional path in their professional life. They pursued a career that, while providing stability and comfort, left them yearning for something more. The daily routine felt like an endless crawl through familiar territory.

However, this individual recognized the signs of change on the horizon. They sensed the restlessness within, the desire for something different, something more aligned with their true passions and aspirations. Instead of resisting this inner call, they chose to embrace it.

Much like the caterpillar entering the chrysalis, this person embarked on a transformative journey. They took deliberate steps to explore new career possibilities, acquiring new skills, seeking out mentors, and networking with like-minded individuals who shared their passions.

As time passed, the changes within this individual became evident. They shed their old career identity and emerged with a renewed sense of purpose and direction. What once felt like a routine crawl through life had transformed into a graceful flight of discovery. Like the butterfly taking to the skies for the first time, they experienced the exhilaration of pursuing their true passions.

Today, this individual thrives in a career that brings them not only financial stability but also deep fulfillment and joy. Their story serves as a testament to the transformative power of embracing change and following one's true calling. This individual is none other than me— James Becton. To find out more about my story visit *James Becton's Rise2Boss*.

The Butterfly's Metamorphosis reminds us that change, though often challenging and uncertain, can lead to beautiful transformations. Embracing change opens the door to new *opportunities, passions, and purposes. Just as the caterpillar becomes a butterfly, we too can experience the thrill of spreading our wings and soaring to new heights when we wholeheartedly embrace change in our lives.*

Antifragility and Change

Change is an unstoppable force that shapes our lives and organizations alike. In this chapter, we explore how adopting an antifragile perspective can serve as a beacon of resilience amidst the storms of change. Instead of merely enduring change, envision a scenario where you harness its power for growth, innovation, and personal transformation.

Consider the mythical phoenix, a symbol of rebirth and renewal. In the face of adversity, this majestic bird doesn't crumble; it rises from its own ashes, stronger and more vibrant than before. Likewise, an antifragile mindset encourages us not just to survive change but to thrive through it, emerging wiser and more resilient.

Our journey includes a captivating story of a struggling business that refused to succumb to a changing market. Instead, it reinvented itself, demonstrating how organizations can embrace change and emerge not just unbroken but revitalized. This tale exemplifies the potential for businesses to become antifragile by viewing change as an opportunity rather than a threat.

Cultivating an Antifragile Mindset

Change often brings discomfort, challenging the boundaries of our comfort zones. Yet, within this discomfort lies the potential for growth, learning, and flourishing, all made possible by an antifragile mindset.

Imagine a blank canvas before an artist—an opportunity to create a masterpiece. Similarly, moments of change can serve as the canvas for our personal and professional growth. In this chapter, we'll explore practical strategies for cultivating this transformative mindset.

An antifragile perspective encourages us to see change as a chance to innovate, to adapt, and to craft a better version of ourselves. It's about embracing the uncertainty, acknowledging that while change may be unsettling, it's also the soil from which resilience and progress can bloom. By adopting this mindset, we not only navigate change more gracefully but thrive because of it, becoming the artists of our own life's canvas.

Change and Relationships

Change doesn't exist in isolation; it reverberates through our relationships, shaping our interactions with family, friends, and colleagues. Antifragility isn't just a personal trait; it's a force that can strengthen the bonds we share with others.

Antifragility fosters adaptability, empathy, and a shared commitment to growth within relationships. When we view change as an opportunity for collective evolution rather than a threat, it can bring us closer, forging bonds that are not only resilient but thriving amidst the ever-shifting tides of life.

Mapenzi Kinege - From Refugee Camp to a Life of Purpose: Mapenzi Kinege's journey from a refugee camp in Tanzania to his current life in the United States is a remarkable testament to the power of resilience and determination. Born near Goma, Africa, Mapenzi's early life was marked by uncertainty, isolation, and poverty.

As an orphan, he faced the harsh realities of life without the support and guidance of a family. Growing up in Nyarugusu refugee camp, surrounded by trees and limited resources, Mapenzi often wondered if he would be condemned to a life of despair like many of the older refugees. The choice between providing for their families or pursuing an education weighed heavily on the young shoulders of those in the camp.

Despite these dire circumstances, Mapenzi refused to lose hope. He understood the importance of (family) community, and the bonds he formed in the refugee camp became his lifeline. These experiences taught him valuable life lessons about resilience and staying motivated in the face of adversity.

When the opportunity to come to America presented itself, Mapenzi faced a heart-wrenching decision. Leaving behind the only world he knew and the people he loved, he embarked on a journey to a foreign land for the promise of a better future. The International Organization for Migration (IOM) provided him with knowledge of American culture and the American dream, but the challenges ahead were daunting.

Arriving in Seattle in 2016 as an unaccompanied refugee minor, Mapenzi grappled with language barriers and cultural unfamiliarity. But his determination to succeed shone through. When asked what he wanted to do next, his immediate answer was to go to school. Education had not been a priority back in the refugee camp, where limited opportunities existed, but now it was his ticket to achieving more.

The path to education for unaccompanied refugee minors like Mapenzi is often fraught with obstacles. Many need additional documents and language support, making enrollment in school a challenging process. However, Mapenzi's American parents recognized his potential and enrolled him in the Seattle World School, where he learned English alongside peers who faced similar language challenges. This supportive environment made all the difference in his educational journey.

Mapenzi's story doesn't end with his successful adaptation to life in America. He pursued a degree in public and global health at the University of Washington, driven by a deep desire to make a difference in the lives of people from backgrounds similar to his own.

Guided by his faith and inspired by his experiences, Mapenzi plans to return to Tanzania after graduation to help (his family) individuals in refugee camps gain access to essential items like soap. He understands the transformative power of even the most basic necessities, which can restore dignity and self-worth to those who have experienced the depths of hardship.

Mapenzi's journey is a testament to the indomitable human spirit. From the refugee camp to the halls of academia, he has used adversity as a springboard to propel himself towards a life of purpose and service, proving that even in the face of the most challenging circumstances, resilience and determination can lead to greatness.

Navigating Organizational Change with Antifragility

In an era of rapid technological advancements and shifting markets, organizations must also learn to become antifragile in the face of change. We'll unravel the strategies that allow businesses not only to survive change but to flourish because of it.

In the organizational realm, change can manifest in myriad forms: mergers, new market dynamics, technological integrations, shifts in leadership, or even global economic fluctuations. Traditional organizational models have often approached change from a defensive stance—how can we minimize disruption, losses, or discomfort? Antifragility flips this perspective on its head, encouraging organizations to not merely survive these disruptions but to thrive because of them.

- **The DNA of Antifragile Organizations:** Organizations infused with antifragility possess certain inherent traits. They have a flexible organizational structure, valuing adaptability over rigidity. There's an inherent culture of continuous learning, where mistakes are not punitive events but learning opportunities. In antifragile organizations, change doesn't break the structure; it informs it.

- **Leadership's Role in Cultivating Antifragility:** The role of leadership in this context cannot be emphasized enough. Leaders in antifragile organizations lead by example, demonstrating resilience and adaptability in the face of challenges. They instill a sense of purpose in their teams, reminding them of the larger goals and visions that transcend transient hurdles.

- **Building Robust Communication Channels:** Transparent communication is the bedrock of navigating change antifragility. It's not enough for leaders to understand and embrace change; this ethos must be cascaded throughout the organization. Open forums, feedback loops, and transparent discussions about organizational changes can minimize resistance and maximize adaptability.

- **Innovation as a Response to Change:** Change is often a harbinger of novel opportunities. While it might pose immediate challenges, the long-term potential for innovation and growth is enormous. By approaching change with a curious mindset, organizations can identify previously unseen avenues for development, expansion, and diversification.

- **Empowering Teams to Be Agents of Change:** Instead of having change directed top-down, antifragile organizations empower their teams to be proactive agents of change. When individuals within a team feel they have agency and can influence the trajectory of change, resistance diminishes, and proactive engagement increases.

- **Feedback Loops and Continuous Improvement:** Antifragile organizations don't perceive change as a one-off event to be navigated and then forgotten. They view it as an iterative process, always seeking feedback, analyzing outcomes, and refining their strategies.

- **The Psychological Dimension:** Embracing change and cultivating antifragility isn't solely a logistical challenge; it's a deeply psychological one. Organizations need to cater to the human aspect of change, understanding and addressing the anxieties, resistances, and fears that come with it. Offering training, building support systems, and creating safe spaces for expression can make the transition smoother and more effective.

In Conclusion

The landscape of organizational dynamics is rapidly shifting. In a world where change is the only constant, traditional models of resistance and survival are increasingly becoming obsolete. The concept of antifragility offers a fresh, invigorating perspective on navigating change—one where challenges are not obstacles but catalysts for growth.

Embracing this perspective requires a paradigm shift, both at the individual and organizational levels. It demands leaders to lead with vision, teams to operate with adaptability, and organizational structures to be fluid and responsive. In doing so, organizations transform from entities merely weathering the storm of change to entities that harness the storm's power to propel themselves forward.

In the words of Bruce Lee, "Don't get set into one form, adapt it, and build your own, and let it grow, be like water." Antifragility in the face of change is akin to being like water—fluid, adaptable, and possessing the latent power to carve through mountains.

The Uncharted Path

In the uncharted territory of change, uncertainty is our constant companion. Yet rather than fearing the unknown, we should embrace it. Change, despite its discomfort, is the canvas upon which our growth, resilience, and antifragility are painted.

Consider the metaphor of a fearless voyager at sea. We cannot control the winds of change, but we can adjust our sails to navigate them effectively. This age-old saying underscores the importance of adaptability and the power we possess to shape our response to change.

Within the heart of change, our antifragile spirit thrives. It's here that innovation takes root, where the seeds of transformation are sown, and where our true potential emerges. By adjusting our sails to the winds of change, we harness the power to not only survive but to thrive in uncharted waters.

The Invitation

Within the pages of this chapter lies more than mere words; it's an invitation to a transformative dance with change. Change, often seen as a foe, is reimagined as an ally in your quest for antifragility. It beckons you to embrace its rhythm, for within its cadence lies the path to unlocking your boundless potential.

CHAPTER
12
THE
UNBREAKABLE SPIRIT

As we reach the culmination of our journey towards antifragility, we stand on the precipice of uncharted territory. This domain is not shaped by the adversities encountered but by the unwavering spirit dwelling within. Our journey has unveiled the latent potential to not merely endure but to thrive amid life's storms. It is a testament to the resilience cultivated, the mindset embraced, and the evolution undergone. In this chapter, we explore the essence of an unbreakable spirit—a spirit that defies odds, surmounts obstacles, and becomes a beacon of inspiration to others.

The Tapestry of Wisdom

As we reflect upon the journey we have embarked upon in our exploration of antifragility, it resembles the intricate threads of a richly woven tapestry, each strand bearing profound lessons. Let us trace our fingers along these threads, rediscovering the wisdom they hold.

Thread 1: Embracing Adversity: We've gleaned that adversity, rather than shattering us, has the transformative potential to forge greater strength, heightened resilience, and profound antifragility.

Thread 2: The Dance with Uncertainty: Uncertainty, once a formidable adversary, has become our dance partner, leading us on a path of growth and unearthing undiscovered treasures.

Thread 3: The Power of Resilience: Our expedition illuminated the symbiotic connection between resilience and antifragility. Establishing resilience serves as the bedrock upon which our antifragile spirit is constructed.

Thread 4: Navigating Relationships: We have witnessed how the principles of antifragility breathe fresh vitality into our personal and professional bonds, transforming them into sources of strength and growth.

Thread 5: Thriving in Career and Business: Antifragility extends its embrace into the professional domain, where challenges metamorphose into steppingstones towards enduring success and perpetual innovation.

Thread 6: The Body and Mind Connection: The fusion of physical and mental well-being constitutes the cornerstone of our antifragile selves. The union of a healthy body and a resilient mind forms an indomitable alliance.

Thread 7: Cultivating Antifragile Habits: Habits, those seemingly inconspicuous daily choices, possess the power to either weaken or fortify our antifragile essence. We have unearthed the habits that nurture strength and adaptability.

Thread 8: The Power of Mindset: Our exploration of mindset has revealed that a growth-oriented perspective harmoniously aligns with antifragility. A mind open to continuous learning can flourish under any circumstance.

Thread 9: Antifragile Leadership: For leaders, comprehending the essence of antifragility stands as a pivotal point. Fostering an antifragile culture within organizations cultivates innovation, adaptability, and enduring success.

Thread 10: Embracing Change: Change, that unwavering companion in our life's journey, transforms into a catalyst for growth and innovation when viewed through the lens of antifragility.

The Unbreakable Spirit Within

In this moment, amidst the tapestry of wisdom woven through our journey, a profound truth emerges. The spirit of antifragility is not a rare gem reserved for the chosen few; it is an intrinsic birthright, a fundamental quality inherent in every individual.

This unbreakable spirit empowers us to confront adversity with unwavering courage, greet uncertainty with genuine curiosity, and welcome change with open arms. It embodies the resolute belief that we are not passive survivors of life's trials but active architects of our own personal growth.

As we take these lessons to heart, we realize that antifragility is not an external force to be sought but an eternal flame glowing within each of us, urging us to embrace life's challenges, dance with uncertainty, and flourish in the face of change.

The Resounding Call to Action

In this chapter, we don't arrive at an ending, but rather a new beginning—an invitation to embark on a lifelong journey of antifragility. It's a call to action, encouraging you to seize each day as an opportunity for growth and to march forward with unwavering strength in the face of life's unpredictable nature.

The stories of those who've ventured toward antifragility serve as symbols of hope, reminding you that within you resides the unbreakable spirit needed to not only endure but to thrive in our ever-changing world. It's a declaration that adversity isn't the culmination of your journey; it's the commencement of your greatest potential.

As we conclude this exploration, may your path towards antifragility be marked by courage, resilience, and an indomitable belief in the power of your unbreakable spirit. Embrace the call, for it is in your continued journey that you'll discover the boundless depths of becoming antifragile.

ACKNOWLEDGMENTS

This book is a testament to the unwavering support and love of my cherished family. To my beautiful wife, Talondia, your boundless encouragement and understanding have been the bedrock upon which I've built this journey towards becoming unbreakable. You've been my steadfast partner in every sense, and I'm profoundly grateful for your presence in my life.

To my five extraordinary children, Aneda, Daisha, Dezmond, George, and Trey (James

III), and my four exceptional grandchildren, Jamya, Aniyah, Addison, and Yara, you are the driving force behind my pursuit of resilience and strength. Your presence fills my life with meaning, purpose, and endless joy.

My gratitude extends to my parents, James, and Jacquline Becton, for instilling in me the values of determination and dedication from an early age. Your unwavering support has been the foundation upon which I've built my dreams.

To my work Dad, Ronnie Miller, who has consistently encouraged me to embrace my potential and allow the divine to guide my path, I extend heartfelt thanks. Your wisdom and mentorship have been instrumental in shaping my journey towards antifragility.

I'm deeply appreciative of the spiritual guidance I've received from my pastor, Bishop Michael Edward Ingram. Your teachings have not only enriched my faith but have also played a pivotal role in my personal development as a minister and a Christian. I'm equally grateful to First Lady Ingram for her constant inspiration and motivation over the years.

To all my siblings, family, friends, and the individuals who are on their quest to become unbreakable and antifragile in this life, you are a source of inspiration and a reminder of the resilience that resides within us all. Your support and encouragement have been instrumental in bringing this book to life.

In closing, I dedicate this work to each one of you, for it is your unwavering belief in the possibility of becoming antifragile that has fueled my determination to explore this profound concept. Together, we embark on a journey towards greater strength, adaptability, and the unshakable belief that, no matter the challenges, we can not only survive but thrive.

With gratitude and dedication,

James Becton